THE POEM HAS TEETH IN IT

AND LIVES IN THE MOUNTAINS

AHSAHTA PRESS
BOISE, IDAHO

THE NEW SERIES
#83

ICON

DAVID MUTSCHLECNER

Ahsahta Press, Boise State University, Boise, Idaho 83725-1525
Cover design by Quemadura
Book design by Janet Holmes
ahsahtapress.org
Copyright © 2018 by David Mutschlecner

LIBRARY OF CONGRESS CATALOGING-IN-PUBLICATION DATA

Names: Mutschlecner, David, author.
Title: Icon / David Mutschlecner.
Description: Boise, Idaho : Ahsahta Press, 2017.
Identifiers: LCCN 2017032284 | ISBN 9781934103784 (pbk. : alk. paper) | ISBN 1934103780 (pbk. : alk. paper)
Classification: LCC PS3563.U855 A6 2017 | DDC 811/.54—dc23
LC record available at https://lccn.loc.gov/2017032284

ACKNOWLEDGMENTS

The author would like to thank the editors of *New American Writing* and *The Colorado Review,* where some of the poems in this book have previously appeared.

FOR ELLIOTT MUTSCHLECNER

CONTENTS

Between Two Candles I	1
Canticle for Our Lady of Guadalupe	11
Eumenidean Etudes	16
The Image of God	22
The Sculptor of Sleep	26
Measures of the Middle Way	28
A Grail for Robert Duncan	30
Easter Vigil	40
Etudes for Karl Jaspers	41
Red Letters	46
Canticle from the Tree of Life	52
From the Icon	58
The Scroll	63
The Vocal Chamber	66
Whose Hand	68
Poem from the Luminous Foyer	70
Einstein's Cross	74
"The Mystery's Festal Garment"	77
Dark Among the Relics	79
"The Roses Had the Look of Flowers That Are Looked At"	82
Between Two Candles II	87
Sources	90
About the Author	91

BETWEEN TWO CANDLES I

In seminar, the older student
put Aristotle to his right
temple, saying *I wish*

I could just feed it all in
—like an Aristotelian app. This hurry
across the hard mammalian spine

of a book. "There must be some book,"
said Keats when dying. Some book
to keep us peaceful and complete

Past present and future collapse
like three sliding cylinders
of a telescope. You might think

that would make you a visionary
—your eye at the center
of perfect convergence, but it only

puts you in a blurred narrow space
I am full of proleptic slips
and impacted questions

—the eye is in the book
as the book is closed
and carried away

Questions come
from a cosmos

of contingency
So the confected

answers come
inexorably from

the same sea. Divinity
cannot be reified

Canyon Road was under construction—
a scooped-out quarter mile—
old asphalt and upturned frozen earth

After midnight mass I ran along
the splayed spine of mammalian ground, crossing
the flashing yellow warning signs

Poem is not only
poem-in-relation

Poem is
relation-in-relation

Its thingness, its
sonorous ontology

cannot be reified
The questions

racing in
to the blackness

break up
and do not

come out
as answers

∽

The book left out in the rain
is sodden and spread,
clumps of pages stuck together, thick

as drunk tongues, talking too much
fumbling through fifty clotted pages
at a time. The sun stiffens

the book without unloosening
the bunches of pages. It could be any
book you know. A five-dollar book

or a hundred-dollar book
It doesn't matter. The rain
will treat all books the same

The language, wrote Williams,
the language is divorced from our minds
The language will treat all books the same

    It is only after
    the holy one is gone

    that the candles are lighted
    Two candles

    with an absence between
    There was no

    linen or book
    while he was present

    It is only now
    that we catch

    the faintly sweet smell
    of beeswax

Tonight Orion's feet
are balanced on the eastern fence
before the world turns

and he ascends, celestial itinerant
in the penultimate
human universe

that has named him. The Ultimate
is saved to save us
from these wind-blown pages

I don't know how they are gathered
into one book, or where
that book is, or how

its lost and uncreated language
does not burn, as Orion's
icy belt burns, our created glyphs

    I wonder at
    the too much

    that keeps us
    before the sea

before the frozen
silence.

∫

Queequeg took up a large book
"and placing it on his lap
began counting the pages with

deliberate regularity; at every
fiftieth page—as I
fancied—stopping for a moment,

looking vacantly around him
and giving utterance to a long-drawn
gurgling whistle of astonishment"

∫

Philosophers cannot
stop writing, and the writing

is a form of talking and talking endlessly
In the loose effusiveness

they sometimes fall, as if by complete
accident, upon a line or two—a few

    words—that really matter
    by which I mean they go into matter, or draw

    therefrom one
    Whitmanaic blade

    Then they go on, in studied
    volubility, talking to themselves

∽

In the huge apartment house
there might be one
narrow window in an outside door—

a few inches
pasted with turquoise crepe paper
And that is all

in the climbing night of a thousand yellow windows
that is all I really look at
—street-level sea-glow of one small page

∽

    Now it is this poem
    that has gone on talking

and I am wondering what might live
between two candles

—silence become
the brick wall

of some apartment house
or the hard spine

of frozen ground
Well then it is

what stops thought
I'm not sure right now

how this hardness
couples or grows

or speaks between
flashing lights or windows

How can anyone wait
to fall down by accident?

CANTICLE FOR OUR LADY OF GUADALUPE

    Dawns
        in my hands
            the little icon:

    pale orange morning
    atmospheric   flat   as the three-inch panel

        Under blood-orange of her robe
        dark folds for shifting
            hips and bending
            knees

Green-black mantle
        shows   scattering
    stars
        half patterned
by the quick breath   of the brush

Smoke-marbled
            fold-flares
    held by
    cloaking night

Her bent head
        crowned with jagged gold
sharp as the patterned thorns
        bordering the panel

            ∽

At turns in her:

        Beatrice
        Athena …

        anamnesis:
        the paired

        resonance of their
        strict thesis

        Where justice
        ghosts grace:

        gray-
        green eyes

The locust tree dreamed
in spiny tufts
of inch-long thorns
purplish against the gray bark, hard
as ironwood

Sangres
    pierced at evening
    drained
in blaze of winter cloud

Night-pale apparition

    How thin
    the body becomes
    made in its own image

~

I lose sight of her
    then see her again
    in measures unforeseen
    by my meantime world

I look
    I don't know where to look
        but looking dares
    look back at me

Sometimes we are severed by
        the very ray
        that pierces us
    so that we go alone

The image of the stone in me
harder than the stony world

~

    Summer was the heavy thunderhead
    arrogated into rain
           beating over heat-
    wrinkled pavement

Love beats and resists
    the golden tone we gave it

A great sweep of shadow
    washes green to black
What is this in me
    not yet me   cast ahead of itself
Who carries the slain voice
    through the night-tongued flame

※

Flaring shadow burns the icon
leaving resonant orange

At eclipse the color drains—skin
ash-thin against

the blinding substance of the light

Smoke no more
    than shadow of smoke

Flesh less dense
        than the blue
        pulse of inbetweenness

What shape   is this
eludes my hands

∽

It is not the poem
        but myself   smoothed
into an afterthought

The poem   has teeth in it
        and lives in the mountains

EUMENIDEAN ETUDES

                        Signal flares
              cross to us
       from Aeschylus

    —our *Ground Work*
    before the next war

These late years, I would rather go
into that second   dark work

under the first   and learn from those furies
whose twisted hands and broken feet

are fouled by Apollonian
vision alone. Loveless

logic of the law,
where is grace

fomented to flame
in the *heart* of justice?

Where is Athena
Who is Athena

       "Listen to my words   which shall never be other than gentle"

                        ∽

Daughters of darkness
I shall not forget

reason hungers in its blown robe—
daylily above

dark violet
Clematis wavers

on the white wall
—soaring thoughts

full of long shadows. A song
      sharp in the snake weed

Yellow yarrow floats through
      huge bursts of Russian sage

Empurpled blood is rayed with thorns   themselves a kind of light

      Clematis
      Clytemnestra

      Cheney's ilk still in the counsels of Agamemnon
      I need tell no one

        the sacrifice
        before the war

        during the war
        after the war

        and after it

                Iphigenias   beyond our count

What conquering in this world is anything but fruitless

    Gangrenous hubris

    Forest of
    dream-stumps

    Daughters of darkness,
    "terrible kindly ones"

    I see you in
    blue-bearded iris like

    some transgendered god

I dream of your gray-eyed
counterpart

I find you
in the corner of the sanctuary
sick with sprayed poison

Child of the earth   Jerusalem cricket

Shiny ocher head
size
of a Russian olive seed.

Body striated like
      a bee's end
        spiraling to a black point

Six legs—just
      two short of a spider—makes

you look
      a venomous threat

yet   benign, slow—
      the heavy head you carry!

Wanting quiet under earth's lid
or behind a wall. Wanting only

    what any seed would want

Child of night
        child   of old gods

deep eyes   under earth's
      eyelid
shunting through
      Eumenidean dark

    We are crawling clearings caught
    in our own tangle

        What rough creature
        slouches

        toward

    We have placed names
    upon a birth—grace

    of bewilderment—clear
    of our words

At times I believe

demon means *demos:*
        the *common* people,

citizens of earth
        but with strange heads—

folded blooms—aporia
        in a thicket of description.

∽

Abrahm:
        "Father of height"
belongs also   to our eyes

        alive in the starry populace

        and yet as often now I would look down
                to find my image—

        "In nature   the furies stir"

THE IMAGE OF GOD

        runs through the wood
        The name in the turn
        of the curving grain

            Write the icon:
            the image of God in words as Word
            proclivities in cursive creaturehood

I learned this on the predella
where language lifts
above itself

        in a spell that wells from every
        given ground gone out
        in waving shapes of earth

            Earth craving
            to its edge with rest-
            less energy

Out of the rags
of words
the poet has no profession,

        he falters, says only
        let altar
        spell Altar

                        I profess to my death
                        as to my Brother
                        my status as

inveterate beginner
and lay down like my Mother
where One

            wells up in the Father
            and pours in braided cords
            of Sisterhood

                     Image of
                                            God
              Image of

                   — so reaching where
                   restless exit is o-
                   pen entrance

Whose face, made less
made more —
mage or

        mirror—taking the name
        burning from Origin
        to the umbrage

            of infancy.
            I speak where One
            is eternally generate

            I speak where the Son
            is speech at work

            ∽

Kindled in the image
"heaven
is the locus of all things"

        Odysseus on Skheria island:
        rag of a man in fetal turning
        Hearth-seed of the cosmos cupped

            under his heart. Ember
            buried in the raked-up leaves
            (What he had pretended

he became) Above the wood
all distance came
to a glittering blue point

in the night's deep hood.
Seraph, your servant-
spark would speak:

> *Image*
> *Image of*
> *Image*

(It is like watching the lips of the loved one
silently reading
guessing at the words)

> Words
> even these
> keep walking backwards
> toward the rippling dark

THE SCULPTOR OF SLEEP

All afternoon I worked on the bronze statues with a steel brush, cleaning off the excess wax that had left a white sheen as of milk or soap streaking in the waves and folds of metal robes, pooling in the pockmarks, pallor sinking into the tooled grooves and flecking the smooth uplifted faces

At five the shadows had fallen so deeply over the sculptured saints that I could no longer work and so went home to my beer and my book. I read and thought of Eckhart: how severe he was, excoriating the soul of every palpable love.

> *All creatures are pure nothing*
> *All creatures have no being*
> *for their being consists*
> *in birth past the ambit of desire*

> > *If it is thus for creation*
> > *can I at least use poetry*
> > *to part the darkness of this*
> > *scabrous abyss?*

> *No, you must walk without*
> *that light, even without*
> *your hands before your face,*
> *without eyes, without hands,*

without face. Poets pretend, but who among us, now or ever, could take the birth-pangs he conceived. Perhaps the cold chill of the metal had turned thoughts feverish: I dreamed I saw, as if under the power of an optometrist's close beam, the back of my eyeball.

        Aching concave membrane
        The same abrasions I had
        clarified in cleaning
        White scales harshly
                        brushed away

The day after the dream I anoint the statues with lemon oil, rubbing the fragrance into fanned-out folds where robe and dress resemble rock faces. Thin chiseled lines and ripples spreading like water blown over rock, oil   into corpse-wound contusions

MEASURES OF THE MIDDLE WAY

In naming God I have named
my desire for God
broken open in the image—

    white limb
    that knows the moon
    before the moon is there—

        winter limb
        bare aspen
        leaning predilection

In the field's
thin hair:
not this

    not that
    let me then
    go with Proclus and

        negate the negation
        —world no longer
        simply nothing

        for even the nothing is gone

Would-be ascendant
vertiginous prayer,　　　first descend

　　　　　beneath all creatures　　and cradle them
　　　　　in words that are naked

　　　　　　　as the first sounds made

　　　　　Matter is measure the sun-gone-moon

Odyssean ember　　　in fetal turning

　　　　　　　　The whole sky sleeps beneath the ocean
　　　　　　　　　　before the sun is born

A GRAIL FOR ROBERT DUNCAN

for Meridian Stephanie Johnson

I

Dante and Virgil
    upon Geryon's back
wheel down in great circles
    toward what Duncan called
"the deep violation"

Inferno, Canto XXXII, lines 124–129

I saw two frozen figures, locked to the neck
in the ice together, the first one's face
against the back of the second one's nape

The first man sank his teeth into the edge
of his companion's skull, his bloody bread
the brain

To eat my own evil
as Geryon might
his venomous tail

Could the skull become
a kind of grail

consuming all
the gall in us?

Anger slaked
for love's sake?

Could grail
and grail

pour back
and forth?

Flow
of sand

from crucible
to crucible

in fiery
mutation?

Could we cut
opacity

     with a streaming
        translucency?

       —if it could be!

"Let it go
   let it go
grief's
  its proper mode"

wrote Duncan
   yet most often we cannot. Duncan could not

    let go   his bitter argument
   with Levertov

   destroying the flow of a life-long friendship
   over questions of poetry
       sublimated into self-
       made war

       To eat   my own evil

   as Duncan might
   his venomous tail

The tail in the mouth is an eternal story
       could we tell it
Old crones at the fire
       We have rattled on forever
and yet I don't know we have told it once
       such that we can leave
through the wound of the nightmare

2

*(After the etching The Well Wisher
by Alexis Palmaffy)*

Doors to
the chest

open like
a tabernacle

swung out
both sides

Within
a cord

noosed about
the bell or

bucket of
the head

Hands
reach in

to pull
the rope

down
so that

in the resounding
chest

a sounding
substance

pours
into space

prepared
for the head

to manifest
heart

Emma Jung writes:

"In order to catch the soul, God created
the *vas cerebi*, the cranium."   Altar

        in the form of a vase
        upturned
        from which

                      a blue light

    Open palm of porcelain

where Anima catches herself

3

"The poet slept within the statue
while the war raged"

        In a time of war
        (all time) hide

        in the hollow of the statue of Venus

        —this seemed to be
        Duncan's sense of it

        as a young man writing
        The Venice Poem

        and it was again, I think, his sense
        in later years

        when he saw Levertov's poetry
        "in the world"

        shorn of hidden self through politics
        And he fought with her as with himself

        unable
        to recall his venom when

        he called her Kali and he struck
        again and again

To speak from the hollow of Love's grail

    amplify the voice of the communion
    of saints, which is now—no other
    Beatific Vision

Yet when he needed
to speak like this to the friend
of his heart   as to himself

        he could not. Did he not
        himself suffer
        a deep violation

      "My sister opens a window in order
        to see   where I am"

        wrote Duncan   when he was dying

Thinking it-
self is
out of order

                    out of order with the time
                    —all its ghostly
                    closed ambitions—

                                          and needs
                                          such a sister
                                          as Robert needs Denise

        Let both

        together open

        the window of my own room

        to see   where I am

EASTER VIGIL

    Who is it looks at me
    through the reflex of a candle flame
    in the polished mahogany

        All that I have done
        flickers in the dark of the not-done
        flickers in the great winged dark

            The hull resonates in the breaking
            swell of the *Gloria*
            The light is sudden   blinding

The world in its age grows godly hollow
What cargo did I dream on
in the long candle readings

        Blown wax
        spatters on the red brick floor
        Any vessel will do

            any hold
            any night to hide the night
            any cistern for the moon

                Any
                sister light

ETUDES FOR KARL JASPERS

        "Thought
                founders
                            upon reality"

    and in its recoil knows
        the quicksilver ground
            the horizon's
jagged signature in lightning

        In flash by
            diaphanous flash
  reason given
                  and taken
    veiled
        averred

It is not by gentleness that I awaken

        ∽

I have been taken
        early on

            by the cipher of the silver
            smoke tree in my night

The pupil of the symbol   opens

∽

When we seek mere object we meet mere illusion

    It is only natural that language lifts the tree

    It is supernatural
    that natural language lifts the tree

The cipher bellies
the figment of measurement

        and yet it lives in the circle of the tree

      —a lattice-filled ovoid
      about which

      my thought
      first orbits

      then weaves

∽

It is a blow to thought
                      when thought passes itself
      breaks
          with itself

        and is an open mote
        a new motility
              —A potent cipher
                      where thought first foundered

∽

When we think we know how to read
that is when the text   seems most oblique

arcane, without title or clue
The names unname themselves

At least we can see and hear again
when we have thrown off like ballast

the pretense of seeing and hearing
Books in trees   layered leaves

—what language
has not been mulched

and yet such
speech we know

palatine in the golden
sun before we go

∽

What is this in thinking
        awakens
        makes ready
        makes
one attentive to One

                shows ways
                    leads
                    the way for awhile
                    before it
too
        falls away
        to another
figure
come alive
        at *this*
        very line
and because of its edge

Thought founders and yet
the afterlight of questioning is gentle. Jaspers

tells me   true questioning is a wooing

        One might woo
the stars

        pursue
the universe with romance

∽

"It is possible to address one another as though in a language which I do not understand as yet but can come closer to understanding without having made it my own"

    Is it possible?

        Can I speak to you
        in a language I hardly know

        yet in my freedom know
        as the speech of your freedom

    Let me cipher
    a leading language in you

Let me speak freely
of what I do not know

and in so speaking
    know you

        freely

RED LETTERS

    I

        I dreamt of them only
            to go through them,

        transfinite in
            the fissures of the holy

        Abide in the cipher
            —liminal
liturgy—
            swings
    as censer

Acrid-sweet
        the incense keeps
Platonic night from seeping into noon
        keeps busy noon from being deemed
                darksome figment of the stars

        And yet one smoke evokes them both
        Erotic body
                Angelic light
        I'm never priest,   but acolyte

        whose thin white taper threads the mass

2

When I dream of poetry

I see the Poem's Body. Moving
       communal limbs
          in touch with the Story

Not that I can touch

nor read   where sentence
                   sleeps
                 with the aleatory

Broken in the cipher script called world
I must not leave
              the line behind   for prose

3.

Sanctuary   laid bare
Cavernous   gray blue
graven stones   ground work   saint-laden

Watch   the moving limbs and smooth faces
      carved into the floor
sweep toward Isaiah's
      watery portal

      Sacristy   open to the wind

Altar   gone
      Priest   absent

A sea-floor stillness at the center of a striking rhythm

Acolyte and janitor, we stood in the narthex
and watched the waves striking
the cliff wall, made of the same
      gray-blue stones, massive,
man sized, gravid with man, worn to smoothness

Heaving water   nearly clear
      as air. Cloudless

churning waves. Depth of the cliff
      by nature and by artifice configured

          transparent to the sea floor

4

      The ancient proof no longer works

         sung outside my head
         in winter grass
         washed red by the stop light

The proof *itself* is radically contingent
      stained by what
      it disdained to take
      up the syllogistic stairs

And yet it works as window

      As icon is open window

Beneathness of blood bequeathed
to the blowing sign

What can I do but outline
the image emptied of its iron

5

Dante and Virgil
                    enter
                                  the *Sacrato Poema*
through the double-arched portal
of the letter M
                    (midway
as we have always been)

illuminated with vines and dark flowers

        Mind

    under sun's *phronesis*

        The signified
        dreams
        beneath the sign. Red letters

        call us   and we go

CANTICLE FROM THE TREE OF LIFE

for Alexis

I

                The woman
                with the star

                above and
                below her

                behold her
                behold her

                above and
                below her

Ponderosa. *Madre*
todoponderosa.   Light

     on towering trunks

    goes deep into quiet power

    And the cottonwoods   full
        of beautiful wind

    On the cusp
           of summer   the Mother

    of God—Sophia   alive
        in green *phronesis*

"Goodness pours into the icon that celebrates creation"

2

    717 AD: an edict, under Emperor Leo
           against the public veneration of holy images
    which John of Damascus fiercely fought

for which he was punished—
        his right hand
                          cut off   and hung
                                                  in public view

        The bloody image   venerated:

                        holy hand
                        reaching down

And John prayed   to *Theotokos*
    that his hand be restored

            and thereafter
                his icon
                of the Mother
                has three hands

                Behold her
                behold her

above and
below her

The woman
with three hands:

two raised, one
lowered. Fruit

from on high

brought down to the roots

3

        Light trembles
                in the leafy mind of God: crown
            above the jagged roots of striding lightning

What work is not imagined
        then seen—   "The Figure of Outward"

        Yggdrasil
            with island heart
    emerald green
    cat eye   flickering
        Beatricean city
    nests in limbs
                overlaid with
      an Assyrian tree—
          patterned   ornate veins
              done outward
                with a neon line—
                darting ruby
                of the mind

4

      Held
           for a moment
                in my descent

  —a netting mesh of moonlight and wind
  transfigured to a thin
  coppery shimmer

Tapered flame
    turns by a dark
    ringed power
    coiling and releasing luminosity

        —a limb of the young ash
           lifts gently
                into the stairwell

FROM THE ICON

    Matter may be nothing
    save form seen inside out

    Form so seen may be
    nothing we have ever seen

          It is always for Aquinas
                        this:

                the gold ground holds
              the halo whose gold
                    bleeds back into the ground

                §

    The scroll he holds
            reads:

                      The bread
                      of angels
                      becomes
                      the bread
                      of men

    The self-

          diffusion of the good. One

                loaf

broken
              into the world

    It is all here

    and yet the *All*
    does not adhere

∽

Halo as in-
    forming breath. *Logos*:

heaven's plenum:
fluid

as the blue line
of earth—ringed

verity our
marriage trace˙

The eyes of Aquinas
clear with the color

of this candor
It is the human

face, needs no
translation

No face
adheres solely

to its given
time and place

Each face
is icon

∽

Halo as
gold gone blue

—a nuptial
relation

The wedding bread was challah

    sweet and heavy dough
    braided thickly

    Brown crust shiny with egg. The rich
    loaf   yellow with egg

You tear a piece off, but see
as you eat it

the pattern
                  of the whole braid

Make of death a Bethlehem:

"house of bread." Earthen substance. Not the world as proof
    of revelation
        from behind the cold curtain
    but world   *as* revelation.   From every limb
        the golden quake of autumn
        to which   from summer's lull
            I wake

"In the word *logos* we hear
 the ringing together of Being and ground"

 Nor groom nor groom's man,   let me be
 the accidental catalyst for beauty

                              twists
         both ways

                         and is consumed

THE SCROLL

    Isaiah lifts the tree-sized candelabra
    soaring twenty feet into the air
    so that the candles touch the falling scroll that holds all

        creatures

        Pleroma
        Plenum
        Plenary
        Sun

    The scroll goes on unrolling past the world
    into the well of anyone's heart. Falling
    into space

        to make space

        ∽

    Why is creation good?

        Because it comes from uncreated Good

    Why do we name the uncreated   Good?

        Because it is the source of all created good

    Why is creation good?

       Swaying

            golden orb weaver
            behind Saint Joseph's
            nesting in the eaves

            I seek her out every
            warm day of autumn
            for her beautiful patience

Swaying

    There is no perfect equivalency
    and yet the scroll goes on

            the wind-
            blown arc

            of a thread
            falling

            Web
            past presence

            (past
            and present)

            shines
            and does not shine

light caught
and released

Line hung
in the pliant

silence

from a high-
beamed order

THE VOCAL CHAMBER

Weekly I clean the great bronze baptismal font, three feet across. The smooth glowing ring of its lip, a hand's span. Across the whole bowl I rub the black off with metal cream, then polish it to a high gloss, then replace the crystal vase, full of freshly poured water, that rests at its kettledrum base. The flaring metal burns with imageless images, the crystal flickers in tongues. The outside of the font is dark and scabrous. Rude cuneiform. A hunted language, half descried

∽

    The curtains   ripple
        as the deacon passes back and forth

    In the wings   the giant dark
        and on the backdrop
        sewn stars

                The moon
                above the air vent

    The bowed shape holds
        a little holy water

            cupped

            and lifted

        from the burnished hollow —
                the cosmos

    The chamber   expands
        for the base   vocable
        breathed

                out
                          as ground upon groundlessness

    Arc of the spoken

            impartable One!

                        —From the mouth of this
                        baptismal font

WHOSE HAND

    The moon descends slowly
    into the terrestrial cleft
    womb long ago she left

        Luminosity spreads into the bowl
        of the valley—curving swath
        of night pale clover

            In the green-black shadow
            light hovers

            The man in the moon in the woman whose moon

                is penumbral inclusion

In the waxen dawn:
Show me where the colors are
and then

        she took the yellow and
        circled my eye with it

            Apollo is forever stupefied
            by light that arrives while his horses
            sleep.   *Gnosis*

is the man in the moon

—so Anima, or some other
voice: *Whose hand*

   circles your eye with the sun?

POEM FROM THE LUMINOUS FOYER

A high-booted man with the moon
in his lap, lambent
crescent outlining

his face. And the long braid
down his back,
like a thick stem or root,

flowers at the end—
night bloom,
half closed

(Alexis tells me the wood block was not of a man but a woman)

"My lord-and-lady-moon"
where image lays down its life for the ground

The man in the moon in the luminous foyer
where the ground pours its life into the image

The image of God as a luminous circle;
inscape the trace of kenotic event

The highest creaturely ring:
the faith that passes all

encompassing,
the faith that may include

God's faith in us, whose breath-
circle softens

hegemonic law
when it covets its own

discoveries. Each lower
circle suffers
                    with the one

                                just
                                above

                                and above,
                                sur-

                                rounding
                                the once-

sharp edges
as if James Turrell
might work

in outer space
Across the dark,
a triangle

of blue light years
whose lines curve,
the sum of whose angles exceeds

180 degrees. Knowing the open
distance, bowed
by breath,

home has
staying power
Lobachevsky's love

bends light and becomes
its own object
when we

step into it—
sheen
of smooth predella,

skeining the distance

In the reflection   of the gauzy blue lamp shade
on the wide-swung   window pane,

starlight   two points

skeining the distance,

a reading
light
where I sit with Gerard Hopkins

What inscapes light but light from light,
nor human nor angelic instress,
but God from God   God-womb:

        the void-motes that
        fill everything,
                free everything

EINSTEIN'S CROSS

for my father

        From a far   quasar

              light
                      bends

              around a closer galaxy: a lens
              training the light to break

              into images
              of the gnostic pulse:

five

coiled   crowns   spoken

out

              spoked with blue fire
              armed with other eyes

              A cross
              inclusive of its visions

              where distance
              is utmost intimacy

                      O we are   companioned

        with many eyes

        Beatific lens

        Striations of night into mind

        ∽

In the refulgent
flood   intensifications
orders that pour

The towering
imaginary water
takes

Isaiah's portal. Hold on
to the sidereal temple
as it breaks
        apart

                wheeling

                    many-eyed

                Heaven

    like the heart

    in the middle

        The soul is more the miracle
        sought out in the scarified
        thorny light

        The universe was easy
        come
        without resistance

            but this   this

"THE MYSTERY'S FESTAL GARMENT"

    Another year I gloss
    the red brick for Easter

        the rag soaked
        and stiffening with wax

            I have polished
            the confessional

            but I do that every where

Blessing earth not
voided by the love of heaven

        Rubbing the black
        grout with lacquer

            Pressing light into the stone

                ∽

            Proof
            follows praxis

                as fact
                follows form

"We know all that!
—what a foolish

       thing to say. Anyone
       can know the story"

but to be present
where love is the form

       to be

       a worker *in* the Work

DARK AMONG THE RELICS

March wind
runs through vents under

      the church
      mixed with highway whine

Cars cut behind
pines near the window. Time

      drawn swift and straight
      breaks against

truncated stillness
Wait in the poem

      where duration cuts
      the line. The mind

handmaid of water
pours over

Between seasons, the substance
changes. The appearance

      stays the same.
      Dark among the relics

I clean beneath the altar
and look up

                                          ∽

Speak into people as into broken bread

        and the bread then nourishes
        past the weight of its grain

holds the whole
as body is held by soul

        Under the appearance of the street called Straight

                a catacomb coil
                              a many-eyed wind.

Bread that breaks
from time

                rises to be read
                as whole.

        Speak into me
        a light transfinite

    at the fissures of poetry

            Fuse-blaze of the inner-outline

    the lifted
             human

Signatory blaze of all   Authorship

    Dark among the relics   I wait

"THE ROSES HAD THE LOOK OF FLOWERS THAT ARE LOOKED AT"

There is something in nature
sentenced in our seeing
A question shines from the corner
of the literate garden:

Can we hope with you?

Apple blossoms in the twilight
and a thousand humming bird moths
Cold cup
       tips at the lip of May. Lilac also
carried in the choir's quilt

There is something in nature that needs
to be here, but to be here
deeply enough so that seeing is leaving—

   So many
       past tally
             in sight's tide

Is there hope in you?

Where the apple tree is catalyst
there is death in the song
it seasons us, leads us even,
we lean on it
much as we do life

Whose hope is beside you?

Quilt and choir. There is something in nature
riven in our seaming lilt

In late April, cold foam
from the fresh-thawed falls
floats over the pool
Green stones below
take the flecked reflections
and turn them into slipping

                              stars

Is there hope besides you?

Thought touches
the curve and core,
morphing the look with the form
that is stored. A star
is the floating reflection
of a rushing conception

Something in nature
is seized in our seeing,
the seizure itself

                    a seeming

Hope through the cloven knowing

        Something in nature
    looks back
waiting and waiting on us

BETWEEN TWO CANDLES II

Why do my thoughts turn
daily in December
to Dante's Buonconte, caught

in a Papal war
whose contention
he little cared for. Cut

mortally, his blood soaked
the bank of the Arno
where his body

fell into the roil of the river
The cross his arms made
over the wound, unloosed

      Torn
      Orphean limbs

      turn
      with rocks and stones and trees

      — kenotic crisis so complete
      God can't recover

      unless the blood and water and oil
      themselves recall Her by another crisis

I was told to clean the case
where the sacred oils were kept—
dead flies under the glass

shelves, shaky on thin pegs
The crystal vase of faintly
greenish chrism oil

tipped, and about two ounces
poured onto the floor of the case
The liturgist was shocked

and said the chrism was as close
to Christ as you could get
barring eucharist.

We soaked
up the oil with towels
to be summarily burned.

> "The great ceiling of the fifteenth century
> is worked with the first gold
>
> brought from America by Christopher Columbus
> and presented by Ferdinand and Isabella
>
> to Pope Alexander VI, who had granted
> them possession of almost all the New World"

The ceiling of Saint Peter's
soaked in blood
We are under the blood

Let the chrism spill altogether out—
grief reading back through the oil-
rich pages of Sheol

        With evening the winter ash
        is bathed in saffron

        while the highest twig
        is tinged with red—

        a quill
        in the freezing air

        where the monk
        can no longer write

        He looks up
        at the smoke darkened face

        of the icon
        and whispers:

        who are you
        who are you

SOURCES

Aeschylus. *The Orestia*. Translated by Ted Hughes. New York: Farrar, Straus, and Giroux, 1999.

John D. Caputo. *The Mystical Element in Heidegger's Thought*. New York: Fordham University Press, 1986.

John D. Caputo. *Heidegger and Aquinas*. New York: Fordham University Press, 1982.

Dante. *Inferno, Pugatorio, Paradiso*. Translated by Robert Durling. Oxford: Oxford University Press, 1996, 2003, 2011.

Robert Duncan. *The Collected Early Poems and Plays*. Berkeley: University of California Press, 2012.

Robert Duncan. *The Collected Later Poems and Plays*. Berkeley: University of California Press, 2014.

Meister Eckhart. *The Complete Mystical Works*. Translated by Maurice O'C Walshe. Crossroad Publishing Company, 2010.

T. S. Eliot. *The Complete Poems and Plays*. New York: Harcourt Brace Jovanovich, 1971.

Paul Horgan. *Rome Eternal*. New York: Farrar, Straus, and Cudahy, 1959.

Karl Jaspers. *Philosophy: Volumes one, two, and three*. Translated by E. B. Ashton. Chicago: University of Chicago Press, 1969.

Karl Jaspers: *Truth and Symbol*. Translated by Jean T. Wilde, William Kluback, and William Kimmel. New York: Twayne Publishers, 1959.

Emma Jung and Marie-Louise von Franz. *The Grail Legend*. Princeton, N.J.: Princeton UP, 1970.

Thomas Mann. *Joseph and His Brothers*. Translated by John E. Woods. New York: Alfred A. Knopf, 2005.

Herman Melville. *Moby-Dick*. Chicago: University of Chicago, 1952.

ABOUT THE AUTHOR

DAVID MUTSCHLECNER is the author of three previous books from Ahsahta Press: *Esse, Sign,* and *Enigma and Light*. He is interested in theopoetics, in which the poetic imagination breathes new life into philosophical theology. In 2011 he received an award from the Fund for Poetry. His first book of prose, *Poetic Faith,* was published by Lune Press in 2016. He lives and works in New Mexico.

AHSAHTA PRESS
NEW SERIES

1. Lance Phillips, *Corpus Socius*
2. Heather Sellers, *Drinking Girls and Their Dresses*
3. Lisa Fishman, *Dear, Read*
4. Peggy Hamilton, *Forbidden City*
5. Dan Beachy-Quick, *Spell*
6. Liz Waldner, *Saving the Appearances*
7. Charles O. Hartman, *Island*
8. Lance Phillips, *Cur aliquid vidi*
9. Sandra Miller, *oriflamme.*
10. Brigitte Byrd, *Fence Above the Sea*
11. Ethan Paquin, *The Violence*
12. Ed Allen, *67 Mixed Messages*
13. Brian Henry, *Quarantine*
14. Kate Greenstreet, *case sensitive*
15. Aaron McCollough, *Little Ease*
16. Susan Tichy, *Bone Pagoda*
17. Susan Briante, *Pioneers in the Study of Motion*
18. Lisa Fishman, *The Happiness Experiment*
19. Heidi Lynn Staples, *Dog Girl*
20. David Mutschlecner, *Sign*
21. Kristi Maxwell, *Realm Sixty-four*
22. G. E. Patterson, *To and From*
23. Chris Vitiello, *Irresponsibility*
24. Stephanie Strickland, *Zone : Zero*
25. Charles O. Hartman, *New and Selected Poems*
26. Kathleen Jesme, *The Plum-Stone Game*
27. Ben Doller, *FAQ:*
28. Carrie Olivia Adams, *Intervening Absence*
29. Rachel Loden, *Dick of the Dead*
30. Brigitte Byrd, *Song of a Living Room*
31. Kate Greenstreet, *The Last 4 Things*
32. Brenda Iijima, *If Not Metamorphic*
33. Sandra Doller, *Chora.*
34. Susan Tichy, *Gallowglass*
35. Lance Phillips, *These Indicium Tales*
36. Karla Kelsey, *Iteration Nets*
37. Brian Teare, *Pleasure*
38. Kirsten Kaschock, *A Beautiful Name for a Girl*
39. Susan Briante, *Utopia Minus*
40. Brian Henry, *Lessness*
41. Lisa Fishman, *FLOWER CART*
42. Aaron McCollough, *No Grave Can Hold My Body Down*
43. Kristi Maxwell, *Re-*
44. Andrew Grace, *Sancta*
45. Chris Vitiello, *Obedience*
46. Paige Ackerson-Kiely, *My Love Is a Dead Arctic Explorer*
47. David Mutschlecner, *Enigma and Light*
48. Joshua Corey and G.C. Waldrep, eds., *The Arcadia Project*
49. Dan Beachy-Quick and Matthew Goulish, *Work from Memory*
50. Elizabeth Robinson, *Counterpart*
51. Kate Greenstreet, *Young Tambling*
52. Ethan Paquin, *Cloud vs. Cloud*
53. Carrie Olivia Adams, *Forty-one Jane Does*
54. Noah Eli Gordon, *The Year of the Rooster*
55. Heidi Lynn Staples, *Noise Event*
56. Lucy Ives, *Orange Roses*
57. Peggy Hamilton, *Questions for Animals*
58. Stephanie Strickland, *Dragon Logic*
59. Rusty Morrison, *Beyond the Chainlink*
60. Tony Trigilio, ed., *Elise Cowen: Poems and Fragments*
61. Kathleeen Jesme, *Albedo*
62. Emily Abendroth, *]EXCLOSURES[*
63. TC Tolbert, *Gephyromania*
64. Cody-Rose Clevidence, *Beast Feast*
65. Michelle Detorie, *After-Cave*
66. Lance Phillips, *Mimer*
67. Anne Boyer, *Garments Against Women*
68. Susan Tichy, *Trafficke*
69. Mary Hickman, *This Is the Homeland*
70. Brian Teare, *The Empty Form Goes All the Way to Heaven*
71. Gabriel Gudding, *Literature for Nonhumans*
72. Susan Briante, *The Market Wonders*
73. James Meetze, *Phantom Hour*
74. Jos Charles, *Safe Space*
75. Julie Carr, *Objects from a Borrowed Confession*
76. Jasmine Dreame Wagner, *On a Clear Day*
77. Allison Cobb, *After We All Died*
78. Rachel Blau DuPlessis, *Days and Works*
79. Kate Greenstreet, *The End of Something*
80. Jen Hyde, *Hua Shi Hua*
81. Lauren Russell, *What's Hanging on the Hush*
82. Sasha Steensen, *Gatherest*
83. David Mutschlecner, *Icon*

AHSAHTA PRESS
SAWTOOTH POETRY PRIZE SERIES

2002: Aaron McCollough, *Welkin* (Brenda Hillman, judge)
2003: Graham Foust, *Leave the Room to Itself* (Joe Wenderoth, judge)
2004: Noah Eli Gordon, *The Area of Sound Called the Subtone* (Claudia Rankine, judge)
2005: Karla Kelsey, *Knowledge, Forms, The Aviary* (Carolyn Forché, judge)
2006: Paige Ackerson-Kiely, *In No One's Land* (D. A. Powell, judge)
2007: Rusty Morrison, *the true keeps calm biding its story* (Peter Gizzi, judge)
2008: Barbara Maloutas, *the whole Marie* (C. D. Wright, judge)
2009: Julie Carr, *100 Notes on Violence* (Rae Armantrout, judge)
2010: James Meetze, *Dayglo* (Terrance Hayes, judge)
2011: Karen Rigby, *Chinoiserie* (Paul Hoover, judge)
2012: T. Zachary Cotler, *Sonnets to the Humans* (Heather McHugh, judge)
2013: David Bartone, *Practice on Mountains* (Dan Beachy-Quick, judge)
2014: Aaron Apps, *Dear Herculine* (Mei-mei Berssenbrugge, judge)
2015: Vincent Toro, *Stereo. Island. Mosaic.* (Ed Roberson, judge)
2016: Jennifer Nelson, *Civilization Makes Me Lonely* (Anne Boyer, judge)

This book is set in Apollo MT and Eurostyle LT type
by Ahsahta Press at Boise State University.
Cover design by Quemadura.
Book design by Janet Holmes.

AHSAHTA PRESS
2018

JANET HOLMES, DIRECTOR

LINDSEY APPELL
PATRICIA BOWEN, *intern*
MICHAEL GREEN
KATHRYN JENSEN
COLIN JOHNSON
MATT NAPLES